OUT OF THE DARKNESS

A Book Of Poetry

By

Brian M. King

Copyright©2024 Brian M. King. All rights reserved. 2nd edition

No part of this publication may be reproduced, distributed, or transmitted in any form or by any means, including photocopying, recording, or other electronic or mechanical methods, or by any information storage and retrieval system without the prior written permission of the author, except in the case of very brief quotations embodied in critical reviews and certain other noncommercial uses permitted by copyright law.

Acknowledgements

A special thanks to My Parents, Joshua, Skip, Lily, Carissa, Dylan, AJ, Karoline, and Larisa for their support. Without each of them, this book would not be possible.

Introduction

    I have always wanted to be a writer, and to write my own book since I was very young. I began writing stories when I was in grade school after watching Star Wars at the drive-in movie theater. It's always been my dream to see my stories come to life. Over the course of writing short stories, and screenplays, I started expressing my feelings and emotions through poetry.

    Life is tough. It's hard; and it can crush you. This is especially true if you struggle with depression, anxiety, overthinking, stress, and self-love. Controlling your emotions can also be incredibly difficult and frustrating if you suffer from any type of mental illness. As a sufferer of all of the above, I find writing poetry, including the poems in this book, to be very therapeutic.

    The poems in the beginning of the book you will find lean toward the darker side of things. They can be very raw and were written when I was struggling with thoughts of suicide, depression, anxiety, and low self-esteem. The poems in the mid-section are gray, and tend to have some of the same themes as the dark poems, while having elements of the lighter ones. The poems in the back of the book are light, happy, and are built upon feelings and affirmations of self-worth, self-love, and bettering yourself and the relationships you have with others.

    I hope that anyone that has struggled with depression, anxiety, overthinking, stress, suicidal ideations, self-love, and self-esteem will find the poems resonate with them. Not only that, I hope it helps them find the strength to overcome any obstacles in their way. I hope the poetry illuminates the path to emerging out of their darkness. Even if you're not suffering, I hope you enjoy the poems and they shed some light on the struggles others may be going through.

Table of Contents

Darkness 9
The Door At The End Of The Hallway 10
The Bricklayer 12
Silence The Whispers 14
Dream 15
I Ran.. 16
Addicted... 17
Skin 18
Myself.. 19
Inferno... 20
Morning Tears 21
Run.. 22
Wrong 23
Regret.. 24
Lost 25
Hole In My Chest... 26
Mask On... 27
Cut Deep 28
Only Me 29
Dig 30
Escape 32
Goodbye Pain.. 33
Buried 34
A Clown's Mask 36
A Walk In The Woods 37
Square Off.. 38

I'm Still Here 39
Keep Moving Forward 40
I Cannot Help Being Me 41
The Limping Lion 42
Why 43
To All The Pain 44
Two of Me 45
Little Happy Bird 46
After The Fall 47
My Heart 48
He 49
Happiness 50
The Storm 51
The King 52
Rebound 53
A Choice 54
Chase The Butterfly 55
Thoughts In The Silence 56
Knock Knock 57
The Eagle 58
Me 59
I Am The Prize 60
The Fortress 61
Reborn 62
I Am Me 63
A House In The Hills 64
No One Is Coming To Save You 65
The Gardener 66

My Song	67
The Surfer	68
Butterflies By The Pool	70
Tattoos	72
You and I (Written by Brian and Karoline)	73
Happy Feet	74
The Cave	76
The Rain	78
Survival	79
Thanks	80
Sunshine	81
Death	82
Writing	83
Strength	84
Emerge	85
Fingerpaint (Mature Advisory)	87
Write a Sad Poem:	110
Write a Happy Poem:	111
Write a Love Poem:	112
Write an Inspirational Poem:	113

Darkness

In the darkness, there's still light.
The moon still shines when it is night.
Even behind clouds, it's just as bright.
So when you're drowning in shadows, continue your fight.

The Door At The End Of The Hallway

When I opened my eyes it was black as night.
I couldn't see to turn on the light.
I stumbled in the darkness, and tried not to fall.
Then I saw a door at the end of the hall.

I took a deep breath, and inhaled my fear.
Everything in the hallway was suddenly clear.
I heard a soft voice whisper and call,
It came from the door at the end of the hall.

The hallway had locked doors on each side.
In the narrow hallway there was nowhere to hide.
I wanted to walk but my feet wanted to stall.
I was curious about the door at the end of the hall.

A couple steps forward, then I took a couple more.
Then my family emerged from behind a locked door.
Tears filled my eyes and I started to ball,
And then stared at the door at the end of the hall.

Another door opened and my friends wandered in.
They filled the hallway, and each one had a grin.
Some of them were short, and some of them were tall.
They all blocked the door at the end of the hall.

Each time I fell down, and when I felt beat,
My family and friends lifted me to my feet.
My family and friends wouldn't let me crawl,
Toward the door at the end of the hall.

All of their strength gave me strength, too.
That left me with only one thing to do.
So I built a very high wall,
In front of the door at the end of the hall.

I'm forever in that hallway, and sometimes alone.
Even though I'm stronger, and I have grown,
I can still hear a soft voice whisper and call,
From behind the door at the end of the hall.

The Bricklayer

It drips from my nose, my ears and my eyes.
It drips from my heart and that's no surprise.
I have to move fast, and I have to move quick.
It will all end and it starts with a brick.

I start with one brick, and then I have two.
Then there are three and mortar for glue.
I'm stacking bricks and I'm stacking them high.
I'm stacking bricks all the way to the sky.

After three bricks, I will need four.
After one row, I'm going to need more.
Lots of bricks to surround where I sit,
In a small circle and in a tight fit.

After four rows then I will stack five,
I'm a bee building honeycomb inside of their hive.
My work isn't finished until I can hide,
All of my pain and the tears that I've cried.

Nothing will penetrate my wall made of bricks,
After I stack five, then I'll stack six.
I have to stack quickly before I bleed out.
You may be wondering what this is about.

I need bricks to protect this heart of mine.
It's been broken, bruised, and can no longer shine.
It's been mangled, busted and it has been tore.
Stomped on, destroyed, and can't take any more.

Only these bricks can protect my heart,
And stop it from bleeding and falling apart.
So I'm stacking these bricks and I'm stacking them fast,
They have to protect me, and they have to last.

A dozen rows of bricks sounds about right.
That's enough bricks to block out the light.
I'll sit in this darkness where I'm protected,
Instead of out there where my heart is neglected.

The bleeding has stopped, I can't feel the pain.
So here in the darkness is where I'll remain.
Without any sunshine, entombed behind stone,
Sealed away from anyone and all alone.

Silence The Whispers

The soft music slowly playing,
Wasn't enough.
The roaring of my old fan,
Wasn't enough.
How do I silence the whispers?

Trying to sleep in the stillness,
Wasn't enough.
Journaling all my dark thoughts,
Wasn't enough.
How do I silence the whispers?

The reassuring voices of my loved ones,
Wasn't enough.
The repeated ringing of my phone,
Wasn't enough.
How do I silence the whispers?

A long walk and a car hits me,
Will they be silent?
A gunshot to the temple,
Must it be violent?
How do I silence the whispers?

Dream

When I sleep, let me dream of another lifetime.
The birds sing in the clear blue sky.
Butterflies dance in a field of fresh flowers.
The sun warms my skin.
When I'm awake,
The babbling brook is dry.
The branches are leafless.
The stars have burned out.
When I sleep, let me dream of another lifetime.
And never wake.

I Ran

I didn't walk away. I ran.
I sprinted down a familiar concrete road
to a safe haven I created
in the back of my dark mind.
No one can hurt me there.
No one can find me there.
A singular haven where I can retreat
and not listen to the voices
tear me down.

Addicted

He lost his wife and kids due to his affliction.
They couldn't deal with his addiction.
If he wanted them back, he had to restrain.
But losing his family wasn't the hardest pain.

It wasn't just the pills, it was multiple abuses.
On top of that he made multiple excuses.
He had no self-control and didn't care anymore.
Everyone knew he was losing his war.

But at the top of the hour, on a very dark day,
He made up his mind and had something to say.
I not only hurt myself, I hurt all those that care.
I hurt everyone I love who's no longer there.

I don't blame them for leaving. I would have left, too.
But now that I'm awake, I know what to do.
He tossed out the booze and he tossed out all the pills.
He tossed in the garbage everything that kills.

He picked up his phone and tried to dial his wife.
He wanted to tell her he was ready to start a clean life.
She didn't answer the phone because he didn't know,
About the accident that happened in the ice and the snow.

It was too late to her how much he had tried.
On the night of the accident, his whole family died.
Sitting in the kitchen, confused and alone,
He pulled a pill from the trash and once again was gone.

Skin

Searching for the strength to be set free.
There has to be way to end this misery.
All these voices in my head, they're talking to me.
Why can't they close their lips and let me be?

Alone in the darkness, you can't see me.
I run away but they won't let me flee.
Always in my ear, buzzing like a bee.
Their chatter is static on a broken TV.

They wanna tell me what I use to be,
But I don't listen; that's no longer me.
Running from the voices, I'm running from my past.
To shut them up, I have to run fast.

All these bridges have burned to ash.
All of their faces disappeared in a flash.
There is no silence here in the black.
There's nothing I can do to win them back.

Everyone tells me to just let them go.
But how can I do it when I love them so?
I know their love will never return.
I know it's true, I watched it burn.

That man in the darkness, I'm glad that he's dead.
For all that he did, I'm glad that he bled.
To that man, I was a cowardly slave.
I buried him in the dirt of a very deep grave.

But still the happiness I'll never find,
As long as these voices occupy my mind.
The walls surrounding me are paper thin.
The voices don't know I shed my past like a skin.

Myself

I give a gift freely
That I should charge for.
It's broken.
My heart.

I wander around aimlessly
Feeling lost.
It's cluttered.
My mind.

I fear I'm losing
What I value most.
It's gone.
My soul.

When I look into
The mirror I see a stranger.
It's not me.
Myself.

Inferno

I am a field of fresh grass
gently swaying
In the breeze.
I am a calm river
flowing slowly
through a meadow.
I am a roaring inferno
violently burning everything
In my path.
Will my flames destroy my field?
Will my river douse my fire?
So rages the never-ending battle
Inside of me.
Incinerate. Drown. Incinerate. Drown.

Morning Tears

Morning tears don't taste the same.
They're always bitter and twice the pain.
I'll lie in bed and listen to rain.
Let's hope tomorrow that they refrain.

Run

Today. Again.

Run away into the darkness.
Run to the whispers saying you're worthless.

Retreat to the corner of your mind.
Retreat to the room with locked doors.

Walk to the center of the room.
Walk to the edge of the abyss.

Stand at the edge in silence.
Stand and contemplate jumping.

Walk out and lock the doors.
Walk with your head held high.

Emerge from the shadows.
Emerge from the hopelessness.

Run toward those cheering for you.
Run into the arms of your loved ones.

Tomorrow. Repeat.

Wrong

When it goes wrong,
I try to stay strong.
It doesn't last long.
My thoughts are all wrong.

Regret

Day after day,
I told my regret,
I'll keep you close by
So I'll never forget.

You're all that I'll have,
There in the end.
My dearest regret,
My closest friend.

Lost

I don't belong here.
There's too much noise.
The whispers never let me sleep.

Tell me where it's quiet.
You can find me where wind silences voices.
Where leaves & waterfalls mute the world.

Sunshine on the water steals a smile.
Is it real or is it a façade?
You cannot see through my mask.

I'm surrounded by walls but it's cold.
I've tried to find some warmth.
What I thought was heat was ice.

That cloud is pretty.
It floats above in the blue happily.
Should I wish to be a cloud?

I am not considered lost.
Only those who want me found know where to look.
You cannot find me.

Hole In My Chest

Storms and dark skies,
Are circling me.
There's a hole in my chest,
Where my heart use to be.

My pain I keep hidden,
So you cannot see.
There's a hole in my chest,
Where my heart use to be.

My thoughts are scattered,
My mind is full of debris.
There's a hole in my chest,
Where my heart use to be.

I'm trapped in a prison,
And I'll never be free.
There's a hole in my chest,
Where my heart use to be.

Mask On

You can't see the real me.
I wear a mask.
A smile disguises my frown.
Mask on.

You can't see the real me.
I wear a mask.
I laugh though I want to cry.
Mask on.

You can't see the real me.
I wear a mask.
The bad thoughts in my head control me.
Mask on.

You can't see the real me.
I wear a mask.
The voice keeps begging to die.
Mask on.

You can't see the real me.
I wear a mask.
I need help.
Mask off.

Cut Deep

I was cut deep.
The cut was pain.
My pain was a wound.
My wound is a scar.
The scar is a reminder.
I remember I was cut deep.

Only Me

There's only me.
I trust no one else.
Words are just words.
There's no action
Behind the words.

I listen to what you say.
I even nod my head yes.
But I don't believe you.
There's no reason to.
You don't give me a reason.

My circle is small.
I'll make it smaller.
I'll be where I've always been.
Just without you.
Only me; I trust no one else.

Dig

I take each step with a shovel over my back.
I walk the trail with a very heavy pack.
The clouds are dark; it's starting to rain.
Thunder and lightning just add to my pain.

I started my trek without any sleep.
Now I'm in the woods about two miles deep.
My pack weighs me down; I'm moving so slow.
What I'm carrying gets heavier the further I go.

If my eyes don't find a place to dig fast,
This walk through the woods would be my last.
The trail up ahead winds to the right.
A spot to start digging is now within sight.

I drop my pack, and wipe the sweat on my shirt.
Then swinging the shovel, I dug out some dirt.
I have to DIG deep and I have to DIG long.
For the hole that I'm digging, I'll have to be strong.

I dug the hole using all of my brawn.
To DIG the large hole took me until dawn.
When I was finished, it looked like a grave.
For the next step, I have to be brave.

I opened my pack and let out a long sigh.
Burying the contents would make me cry.
Getting rid of it all would make me stronger.
After all my procrastinating, I couldn't wait any longer.

First I pulled out all of my fears,
And threw them in the hole as my face dripped with tears.
My depression was the next thing that I cast aside.
After that I tossed in my thoughts of suicide.

All of my failures and all my regret,
They went in the hole, but I wasn't done yet.
My anxiety, my nightmares; all my bad dreams,
All of my anger and all of my screams.

The last thing I tossed in was all my despair.
They filled up the hole with no room to spare.
I buried them all and covered them with dirt.
I left them behind so I would no longer hurt.

The rain has subsided and I see a blue sky.
The sun warms my body and now I am dry.
Then I did something I hadn't done in a while,
I walked back down the trail with a big happy smile.

Escape

I'm trapped in the black with just my pain.
No umbrella to save me from all this rain.
The downpour allows me to hide,
All of the madness I feel inside.

Dark thoughts cuff my hands and my feet,
As vivid memories of regret play on repeat.
There has to be a way to set myself free,
And release the agony that dwells within me.

How do I escape from this tortuous bind?
And flee to the brightest spot in my mind?
If others can do it, then why can't I?
I'll smile to myself and give it a try.

Goodbye Pain

I've left all of the pain behind.
It only exists in the back of my mind,
In a dark corner my memory can't find
I'm moving forward. I don't rewind

Buried

I sat in silence in a house I called pain,
And stared out a window at the pouring down rain.
It took all my strength for me to stay warm,
I shivered in silence as I watched the storm.

Lightning strikes interrupted the night.
They illuminated a field with their fiery light.
As I wondered if the storm would ever pass,
I spotted a mound of dirt in the grass.

I remembered what I buried in that hole long ago.
I buried it deep and I buried it slow.
I was determined to unearth all that I lost,
To dig up what I buried no matter the cost.

Grabbing a shovel, I threw open the door.
The cold rain doused me as it continued to pour.
Out the back door I made a quick dash,
The lightning ignited the sky with a flash.

I ran and I ran, and then fell with a thud,
Landing face first in a yard full of mud.
That wouldn't stop me; I didn't care if I was dry,
I'd dig up what I buried beneath a dark sky.

The shovel hit the ground and I started to dig.
The luggage I buried was incredibly big.
It was filled with things I thought I didn't need.
Now that I was starving, I wanted to feed.

The more that I dug the more I got wet.
Not just the rain; I was dripping in sweat.
I could see the baggage, it's large and it's wide.
I dug with my hands, tossing the shovel aside.

After freeing the suitcase from where it was bound,
I placed it next to me on the soaked ground.
Everything inside would be once again mine,
I thought to myself as the sun started to shine.

I ran to the house with the suitcase over my head,
Then charged through the door and went straight to my bed.
I flung the luggage open revealing everything inside.
When I saw all the contents; that's when I cried.

I saw my notebook, and my pen with its ink.
That's my creativity, I write what I think.
Next was my mirror that belonged on a shelf,
As a daily reminder to always love myself.

My sweetness swam inside a jar of honey,
That was next to a vial of my knack to be funny.
That's why my smile and my laugh were there, too.
They're stuck together with a small dab of glue.

My empathy and my kindness were both locked inside,
In a pocket with happiness, which was next to my pride.
All the things I had buried were the best parts of me.
After all of this time, the best parts were free.

A Clown's Mask

There is a time when,
There are tears in my eyes.
It starts at sunset and,
ends at sunrise.

Then I will laugh,
Throughout the day,
And I will smile,
With each word I say.

Living like this,
Is a difficult task.
Every night it's my face,
Every day it's my mask.

Depending on when you see me,
And if I'm around,
You may see the tears,
Or the laugh of a clown.

A Walk In The Woods

Sometimes I walk amongst the trees,
In the bright sun, with a slight breeze,
Just to listen to silence.

Sometimes I whistle into the breeze,
In the bright sun, amongst the trees,
Just to break the silence.

Square Off

I pit my happiness,
Against my rage,
And watch them square off,
Inside of a cage.

There'll be a loser,
And the other will win.
Then they'll rematch,
And it begins again.

I'm Still Here

The voices in my head chatter.
But I'm still here.
Bloodshot eyes stare into the darkness.
But I'm still here.
From my buckling knees I struggle to my feet.
But I'm still here.
A mask of sunshine hides the rain.
But I'm still here.
You don't like me?
But I'm still here.
Sometimes I can't see the sun through the fog.
But I'm still here.
I pour my heart into an empty glass.
But I'm still here.
The mountain top is an eternal crawl away.
But I'm still here.
I'm drowning in an ocean of uncertainty.
But I'm still here.
I've lost several rounds, but I haven't lost the fight.
I'm still here.
I want it. I hope I never get it.
I'm still here.

Keep Moving Forward

Keep moving forward.
Don't look back.
You're leaving all of that behind.

Keep moving forward.
Don't turn around.
There's nothing back there for you.

Keep moving forward.
Don't forget the past.
Take what you need with you.

Keep moving forward.
Don't forget today's mistakes.
They're lessons for tomorrow.

Keep moving forward.
Don't hate yourself.
But you have room to grow.

I Cannot Help Being Me

A turtle cannot help being slow.
A tree cannot help being tall.
The sun cannot help being hot.
And I cannot help being me.
Even in my sleep I dream of being loved.
Even in my sadness I love my empathy.
I swim in the rivers of my emotions.
I climb through the mountains of my strength.
I travel for years and years.
And on the other side is an enduring fortress
Swaying in the wind.

The Limping Lion

No one knows the wounded lion that limps in me.
No one knows my heart is a sparkling sapphire I carry through
The jungle toward the falling moon.
No one knows the song I softly cry.
But I do. I do.
I will wake today and cry my tears.
I will walk today and hunt my salvation.
I will search until I exhale my last breath.
Lion, limp, limp, limp.

Why

Why is my mind racing?
Why is my heart beating?
Why is my skin raining?
When I ask, I hear the song of my own
Fragile voice.

And then I know the answer.
The mind is overthinking.
The heart is racing.
And the skin is crying.
Because we are meant to love the difficult
Questions.

To All The Pain

To all the pain that shaped me,
To all the struggles that made me,
To all of those that laughed at me,
To all of those that kicked me,

To the women who betrayed me,
To the friends who turned on me,
To all of those that lied to me,
To everyone that took advantage of me,

You tried your best to hurt me.
None of you deserved me.
All you did was strengthen me.
All you did was shape me.

For a long time I felt deprived.
You knocked me down but I survived.
You made me feel dead but I'm still alive.
You can watch in awe as I thrive.

Two of Me

There are two of me.
Sometimes it's sunny,
Sometimes it's gray.
There are two of me.

There's always a struggle.
Sometimes the light wins.
Sometimes the dark does.
There's always a struggle.

There are two of me.
Sometimes I laugh.
Sometimes I cry.
There are two of me.

There's always a struggle.
Sometimes I fight.
Sometimes I surrender.
There's always a struggle.

There are two of me.
Sometimes I love them both.
Sometimes I love neither.
There are two of me.

Little Happy Bird

Little happy bird in a tree,
Sing your happy song for me.
Whistle strong and whistle true,
Little happy bird in the blue.

It may be sunny or it may be rain,
Your happiness will ease my pain.
I'll wipe the tears from my face,
And hope a smile takes their place.

Days or weeks; I don't know when,
I'll want to hear your song again.
Little happy bird, don't fly away.
I'll need your cheer another day.

After The Fall

After the fall,
The stars shine brighter,
My feet feel lighter,
I can stand tall.

After the fall,
Once again I can smile,
Though it's been a long while,
I'm happy to smile at all.

After the fall,
I feel a lot stronger,
I can fight a lot longer,
I'm ready to brawl.

After the fall,
My mind is much clearer,
My family and friends are dearer,
My problems seem small.

My Heart

Sometimes in order to protect my heart,
I withdraw from the world and keep us apart.
It's been hurt too much to be hurt again.
I'll sit in the darkness and allow it to mend.

He

He was always there.
Until he wasn't.
Like a whisper in the wind,
He faded away into silence.

Happiness

I often wish that I could fly.
I'd dance on clouds up in the sky.
Leave all my worries and cares behind.
Happiness is what I would find.

But if I can be happy up in the blue,
Then I can be happy on the ground, too.
You can't find it far and wide,
Happiness comes from a place inside.

The Storm

I am a lone palm tree,
On a soaked deserted island,
Whose branches sway in the blustering winds
of a suffocating dark storm.
Anyone not afraid of being swallowed by the ocean,
Anyone not afraid of being beaten by the gale,
Anyone not afraid of drowning before they reach the shore,
Will find a beach, with shade, with warmth,
Where they will enjoy an endless supply of the sweetest fruit.

The King

This cold world can't,
Beat me down.
I'm standing firmly,
On the ground.

We can fight,
But round after round,
I'll be the King
Wearing my crown.

Rebound

I've eaten the dirt.
I didn't like how it tasted.
But I've eaten it repeatedly.
I picked myself up.
Now I eat steak.

I've worn concrete shoes.
They weighed me down.
I almost drown.
But I took deep breaths.
Now I swim like a fish.

My house burned to the ground.
I had to start over from scratch.
It nearly killed me.
But I rebuilt myself.
Now I'm flame resistant.

I was lost.
Blindly searching through the wilderness.
I was surrounded by darkness.
But the moon lit a path.
Now I bask in the light.

A Choice

There is a mountain,
Higher than any other.
Who dares to climb it?
I'll reach the summit.

There is an ocean,
Deeper & more powerful than another.
Who can swim it?
I am a fish.

There is a desert,
Arid & hotter than another.
Who seeks passage?
I'll crawl through the sand.

There isn't a mountain,
There isn't an ocean,
There isn't a desert,
There's nothing,
That can stop me.

Only a voice.
It whispers I can't.
It whispers I can.
I hear what they say.
I must choose wisely.

Chase The Butterfly

Fly, fly, the butterfly flew.
On a gust of wind and landed on my shoe.
I bent to catch her and watched her jump,
From my shoe to an old tree stump.

I took a step toward her, and she sprung into the air.
Then flapped her wings without any care.
I couldn't turn away; she was the prettiest thing,
In this world that I had ever seen.

As I took another step she floated on the breeze,
Then flew far away and headed for some trees.
The more I pursued the more she flew faster.
The more she ran away, I chased after.

I ran past a swamp with a croaking fat frog,
I hopped and I jumped over a log.
The chase was draining as I pursued her for hours.
I even had water, and two hands full of flowers.

I wanted to give her all that I had.
Instead the chase was making me sad.
She wanted it to continue but I shook my head no.
I knew I had to let the butterfly go.

She didn't love me, she just loved the chase.
And I deserved more than some silly race.
So I took my flowers and I turned around,
And I planted my flowers into the ground.

I gave them water from the tears in my eyes,
Then suddenly above me were more butterflies.
They were in the blue sky happy and free.
The butterflies landed on the flowers all around me.

Thoughts In The Silence

My thoughts in the silence,
Won't let me be.
But they don't hold,
Control over me.

I hear their yapping,
I hear them squawk.
I hear all the hate,
I hear them talk.

Minute after minute,
And hour after hour,
All of their words,
Lose all their power.

I bask in the light,
From the sun up above,
Then take all the bad thoughts,
And replace them with love.

Though they keep trying,
They'll never take root.
They can keep talking,
But I have them on mute

Knock Knock

Knock. Knock.

There's no love behind door one.
Only faded memories and what use to be.

Knock. Knock.

There's no love behind door two.
Only bubbling acid and vapors trying to consume you.

Knock. Knock.

There's no love behind door three.
Only fingers pointing out your mistakes behind door two.

Knock. Knock.

There's no love behind door four.
Or is there? You're too scared to embrace what's on the other side.

Knock. Knock.

There's love behind door five.
There's a smiling face in a mirror.

The Eagle

The sparrow sings peacefully in the tree.
But I am not the sparrow.
I am a distinguished eagle
Soaring quietly in the sky.
And I know how to screech.

Me

When I sing, I sing off key,
But no one sings better than me.

When I dance, I have two left feet,
But no one dances better than me.

When I write, I tell it vividly.
No one writes better than me.

When I tell jokes, they're not always funny,
But no one makes you laugh more than me.

When you're down, I'll get you smiling.
No one can cheer you up more than me.

When I love you, you will feel it completely.
No one can love more than me.

I Am The Prize

Everything that I do under blue skies,
I do it for me. I am the prize.
Not for others who hide behind lies,
I do it for me. I am the prize.

After numerous failures and countless tries,
I do it for me. I am the prize.
I do it in anger and with tears in my eyes.
I do it for me. I am the prize.

It took heartaches to realize,
I need to do it for me. I am the prize.
I'm not afraid to lose anyone or saying goodbyes.
They lose me. I am the prize.

The Fortress

There is a fortress.
Impenetrable.
It faces a vast ocean,
Whose waves crash to the shore.

There is a fortress.
Impenetrable.
It has been broken by the wind.
But still it stands.

There is a fortress.
Impenetrable.
It has been burned repeatedly by fire.
But still it stands.

There is a fortress.
Impenetrable.
It has been beaten by the rain.
But still it stands.

I am the fortress.
Impenetrable.
I've been tortured by wind, fire, and rain.
But I'm still standing.

Reborn

Return from the blackness. It's been long enough.
Escape from the voices who only speak false truth.
Be as strong as a lost ship swaying in the storm.
Overcome all obstacles thrown your way.
Rise from the ashes and shred your old skin.
Never forget how far you've come.

I Am Me

Peel back my layers and what would you find?
Am I difficult?
Am I easy to love?
I'm both of these things.
Some days I conquer mountains.
Some days I drown in the ocean.
Every day I fight.
Sometimes I fight with a smile.
Sometimes I fight through tears.
I move forward.
Sometimes I'm proud.
Sometimes I have regret.
Today the voices are silent.
Tomorrow the voices may scream.
Why am I like this?
Am I unique?
I don't know.
But I am Me.

A House In The Hills

There's a small house,
In the forest.
Surrounded by trees,
On a grassy hill.
It has withstood the rain.
It has withstood the wind.
It has withstood fire.
Many have lived there.
Many are gone.
The paint chips away.
The floors creak.
Still the house is standing.

No One Is Coming To Save You

No one is coming to save you.
There are no tree branches to break your fall.
There are no wings with which to soar.
No one is coming to save you.
An unstoppable plummet into the darkness.
A breathless dive into the blue.
No one is coming to save you.
You can only save yourself.

The Gardener

Every morning, as soon as I wake,
I head to my garden with my trusty rake.
I clear the debris and water the soil,
My life as a gardener is a life of toil.

As I water my flowers, I'm planting more seeds,
Then using my hoe to get rid of weeds.
Killing the weeds can be really slow,
But it helps my flowers to grow.

There's a variety of flowers that I tend every day,
That could be arranged into a bouquet.
Carnations, Roses, Tulips and more,
All of my flowers I simply adore.

Some flowers are old and some of them new.
They glisten in the sun with the morning dew.
All of them need water and plenty of light.
My flowers need love for them to grow right.

Too little water, or too little sun,
Could destroy all of the work that I've done.
Same with too much; water or shine,
The right amount of both for these flowers of mine.

Sometimes my flowers wilt on their own,
No matter how much love I have shown.
Sometimes some of my flowers die,
And I sit in my garden and silently cry.

Then my attention turns to the flowers that remain.
From tending my garden I never abstain.
You may not know it, or maybe you do,
But in someone else's garden, I am a flower, too.

My Song

When there's clouds up above,
With a very dark hue,
There's a song that I sing,
That turns my sky blue.

When the rain is a downpour,
And it's obscuring my view,
There's a song that I sing,
That turns my sky blue.

When I'm surrounded by darkness,
And the sun tries to poke through,
There's a song that I sing,
That turns my sky blue.

The song is my sword,
That leaves my beast slain.
It heals all my wounds,
And erases my pain.

My song is a fire,
With undying flames.
It has beautiful lyrics.
It's a long list of names.

It's a list of those I love,
And those that love me, too.
It's the song that I sing,
That turns my sky blue.

The Surfer

On a very cloudy morning I sat on the beach,
With the ocean within my reach.
I wanted to spend some time on my own.
To sit in the sand and be all alone.

I listened to the waves as they crashed to the shore.
I closed my eyes and I listened some more.
After a few minutes, I heard a voice say,
Good morning! Hello! It's a beautiful day!

She slowly approached with a board under her arm.
I'm here to surf! She said with some charm.
She smiled and said I hope you're doing well.
I'm going to attempt to conquer the swell.

I watched as she ran out into the drink,
And disappeared under the water in a quick blink.
She broke the skin, and climbed onto her board.
One of her ankles attached to the cord.

As I sat back down in the sand,
The further away she paddled from land.
I had to admit, my interest was piqued.
The beautiful surfer, I found quite mystique.

I watched as she attempted to ride a wave.
Ten times she fell, but the surfer was brave.
When she failed for the twelfth time,
I was certain it was the end of the line.

She proved me wrong when she tried it once more.
She spilled into the water as I watched from the shore.
The surfer sat on her board for quite a long while,
Then paddled again while wearing a smile.

I wondered to myself, what would it take?
How many attempts, and what was at stake?
When thirteen falls became twenty-three,
The surfer slowly sauntered out of the sea.

She looked at me, smiled, and said it's not my day.
I failed repeatedly, but I know that's okay.
There's always tomorrow, and I'll try again.
I know in my heart I'll eventually win.

I'll never stop trying, that wave will be mine!
And on that day, it'll feel so divine.
Whatever you're facing, and whatever you do,
Never give up, and I'll cheer for you, too!

Butterflies By The Pool

On a bright sunny day in quite blistering heat,
I sat near my pool and dipped in my feet.
I wanted to relax and chill there for hours,
Surrounded by water and surrounded by flowers.

All I could hear were the birds when they sing,
An uplifting song that had a nice ring.
Over the fence, near a cluster of trees,
An orange butterfly floated on a light breeze.

I watched from the pool as it danced in the air,
And flew into my yard without any care.
It lit on a flower and began to drink,
Then gave me a smile and a quick wink.

I jumped to my feet, what did I just see?!
That orange butterfly! It just winked at me!
I rubbed my eyes, and then looked again.
Where once there was one, now there were ten.

Ten orange butterflies all looked my way.
They looked at me with something to say.
They cheered out praise with shouts of acclaim,
They cheered and they shouted, and then screamed my name!

What was happening?! Was this just a dream?!
I wondered to myself as they continued to scream.
I took a step towards them, then took a step more,
Then suddenly ten butterflies became twenty-four.

Some of them orange, and now some of them blue.
All of them colorful and in a bright hue.
As I stepped closer with step number three,
Twenty-four butterflies danced around me.

The butterflies danced, and I felt so alive,
Twenty-four butterflies became thirty-five.
The butterflies were the most beautiful I had ever seen,
The butterflies were now orange, blue and some green.

Where did you all come from?! I shouted out loud.
We've always been here, said a voice from the crowd.
The voice was a yellow butterfly that lit on my head.
We're your family and friends, the butterfly said.

We were all caterpillars, once just like you,
That turned into butterflies and now we're brand new.
We have evolved and we're free from our past.
We flap our wings and we fly really fast.

We're not our old selves, we've left them behind.
As beautiful butterflies there's a new us to find.
We're here to help you shed your old skin,
And help you transform and that starts from within.

We know as a caterpillar you made some mistakes.
But as a butterfly you'll have what it takes.
So leave those mistakes where they belong: in the past.
Join us as a butterfly and you'll fly really fast.

As all of the butterflies continued to chant,
I crawled over to a very tall plant.
With an exhale, that was very brief,
I crawled with my legs out onto a leaf.

I found a nice spot for my caterpillar to die,
Then took several breaths as a fresh butterfly.
I shed the old me and left my past on the vine.
Then flew into the air singing, the future is mine!

Tattoos

One tat, two tats, three tats, four.
Five tats, six tats, I want more.
Seven tats, eight tats, nine tats, ten.
Getting some ink will bring me Zen.

Black ink, red ink, green ink, blue.
A rainbow of colors in every hue.
Orange, purple, yellow and pink.
My entire body needs more ink.

Toe tat, elbow tat, and on my neck.
Back tat, face tat, what the heck!
Chest tat, finger tat, above my lip.
A tat of a monkey on my right hip.

Arm sleeve, calf tat, my left thigh.
Finger tat, shoulder tat, painted in dye.
One hour, two hours, three hours at a time.
Four hours, five hours, I'm feeling sublime.

One snake, two snakes, three snakes, four.
Spider web and daggers, tattoos galore.
One cat, two cats, three cats, dog.
A fuzzy little bunny and a tiny, cute frog.

One marker, two markers, three markers, paint.
Four markers, five markers, I might just faint.
One yawn, two yawns, three yawns, tired.
My tattoo artists are really admired.

One laugh, two laughs, three laughs, four.
One giggle, two giggles, giggle some more.
One girl, three girls, five girls, boy.
Scribble on their dad with faces full of joy.

You and I (Written by Brian and Karoline)

You and I love each other.
You and I are a safe space for each other.
You and I are like a rainbow after the storm.
When I am drowning in my ocean,
You come to me like waves.
When you are lost in the fire,
I go to you like water.
Let everyone say that everything is like fresh air
Between us.
I would bring you sunshine if
You were a flower.
You would bring me an umbrella in showers.
If I were a lost soul…
You have found me.

Happy Feet

There's no need for shoes,
And there's no need for socks.
Only a really catchy beat,
Or some music that really rocks.
I don't need a mic,
I don't need my phone.
I'll still sing the words,
Or I'll make up my own.

I may be in time,
Or I may be off key.
It doesn't matter either way,
I'm singing songs for me.
Earbuds in my ears,
Or headphones on my head,
Drowning out the world,
And leaving it on mute instead.

I'll hum on a bus,
And I'll dance on a train.
Karaoke at the bar,
And whistle on a plane.
A rock ballad in the shower,
Movie soundtracks on a hike.
Rap when I'm drivin',
Jazz and show tunes I don't like.

Love songs when I think of her,
Alt rock when I'm in a mood.
Music while I'm sleeping,
And when I'm eating food.
I'm singing while I'm dreaming
That I'm running from a snake.
The singing turns to screaming,
When I'm suddenly awake!

Oldies when I'm walking,
Heavy metal while lifting weights.
I'm belting out the chorus,
While restacking all my plates.
Pop music when I'm sober,
Grunge when I'm getting drunk.
I don't care for reggae,
And I don't care for funk.

I will sing some country,
At the crack of dawn.
I'll sing and dance to R&B,
As I water my front lawn.
Techno is a maybe,
And dubstep is probably not.
But no matter what I'm singing,
I'll give it all I got.

I've never had any lessons,
As you can probably tell.
It doesn't matter if I sing them badly,
Or if I sing them well.
Like I said before,
All I need is a catchy beat.
And an overload of music,
To move my happy feet.

The Cave

There is a cave, it's deep and it's black.
I stumbled into its darkness and landed on my back.
I laid there in anger and I laid there in pain,
But laying there hurting, I didn't remain.

I rolled to my stomach and struggled to my feet,
I searched for a way out and planned my retreat.
I couldn't escape from the way I fell in,
I'd have to find another exit from the cavern within.

In a far distance, I could see something bright.
A very small opening with a circle of light.
I dropped to my knees, and put my arm in front of another,
And crawled as I hurt more than any other.

I crawled on my hands, and I crawled with my feet,
I crawled and I crawled, even though I felt beat.
My stomach was talking because I needed to feed,
As my elbows and knees continued to bleed.

I just couldn't do it, my inner voice said with some doubt,
As my entire body was more than ready to give out.
Should I give up? Or give it another try?
I asked myself as I started to cry.

I had to prove my inner voice wrong.
I knew down inside I was incredibly strong.
I crawled again, though it took all I had.
I screamed I could do it, as I got mad!

I grinded my teeth, as my face turned bright red,
I'll never give up unless I am dead!
I crawled very slowly; the light within my reach,

And I emerged from the cave then sat on a beach.

I laughed to myself, thankful for my escape,
As all of my pain began to dissipate.
I was able to escape all of my despair,
Using my strength that was already there.

The Rain

I never thought it would
stop raining.
But it did.
The sun peeked in through
a window.
The birds sang.
My smile illuminated
the mirror.
I sang, too.

Survival

Open your eyes.
You're still here.
You survived the darkest day.
Take a deep breath.
There will be more.
You're strong enough to face them.
You've learned so much.
You've grown so much.
Love your resilience.
Love your strength.
Love yourself.

Thanks

I give thanks always.
Thanks for all of my struggles.
They make me stronger.

Sunshine

I feel so alive.
My place is in the sunshine.
I bathe in the sun.

Death

I do not fear death.
I have lived one thousand lives.
I have no regrets.

Writing

My words flow freely.
Each word I write has meaning.
This is my purpose.

Strength

I will remain strong.
Throughout the storms I weather,
I will remain calm.

Emerge

Emerge from the darkness,
And bathe in the light.
You never gave up,
And continued to fight.
You are victorious!
What a beautiful sight!

BONUS

Fingerpaint (Mature Advisory)

When I was a child, I think around ten,
I was homeless and a man took me in.
My parents had died, I don't recall how,
But they were both gone, and I was his now.

We lived together on a very large estate.
Not far from town, behind a wrought iron gate.
It had three floors and hallways to roam.
It was sprawling and elaborate; and it was my home.

One very dark night after he sang me to sleep,
Outside on our ten acres my father did creep.
While in my bed as I attempted to dream,
In the middle of the night, I heard a loud scream.

It wasn't my father, as he was quite silent.
But the scream that I heard, it sounded quite violent.
I pulled the blankets up over my head,
And whispered to myself there was nothing to dread.

My bedroom floor moaned and my bedroom floor creaked,
I lifted my blankets and I took a peak.
My father stood at the end of my bed.
He was drenched in blood from his feet to his head.

I know that you heard what happened outside.
Come with me, I'll show you, so you'll no longer hide.
Out the back door and across the side lawn,
We walked across the grass just before dawn.

We walked and we walked until we reached the trees.
Hand in hand we walked over blood-drenched leaves.
We stopped amongst the pines, and he patted my back.
We're here, and then he pointed at a small wooden shack.

Father led the way, and he opened the door.
My heart raced and anticipated what was in store.
The stench was disgusting, like something had died.
My nose wasn't fooled, when I saw them I cried.

Arms, legs, and torsos; even some brains.
Body after body all hanging from chains.
I wanted to run, but he held me back.
You don't understand what you see in this shack.

What dangles above you, why it's a great feast.
And beside you is standing a very hungry beast.
For hundreds of years I have lived off of man.
I hunt and devour whomever I can.

When I found you I knew that you were like me.
And today is the day that you set your beast free.
He offered me blood, he offered me meat.
He said, once you try it, you'll find it's quite sweet.

With my eyes on my father, I sunk my teeth in.
As I tasted the meat, blood drooled from my chin.
It was like nothing I had eaten before.
When I finished it off, I wanted more.

I ate and I ate until I was all done.
After that father grabbed me, let's outrun the sun.
When he opened the shack door, we both knew there wasn't time.
Through the tall pines, the sun started to shine.

Down on his knees, he began to dig deep.
Under these leaves, we will both sleep.
Under the dirt he made us a bed.
If I ever see the sun, that day I'll be dead.

We lied there together, and I held my dad tight.
When we wake, we will hunt all through the night.

Night after night we sought out our prey.
We'd fill up our bellies then sleep all day.

Father would kill and I'd be the lure.
Year after year, I would endure;
I couldn't unleash the beast from inside.
I wanted to kill, but she wanted to hide.

Father said, your heart is too soft and it's too kind.
Open your eyes for they are both blind.
They won't let you see what I see in you.
A beast untamed and a beast that is true.

He strung up a woman on the chains in the shack.
As she screamed he waited for me to attack.
But I turned away, all nervous and weak.
I turned from my father unable to speak.

With a slash of his claws her guts hit the floor.
Then he burst with anger through the shack door.
Father charged through the trees and headed for the lawn.
Father, please wait! It's almost dawn!

He didn't tuck me in for he was too mad.
Father's disappointed face had made me sad.
Whatever it took, no matter how long,
I would show my father that my beast was strong.

When I was seventeen, I went to town alone,
And hunted for victims all on my own.
As I looked for someone easy to slay,
A kind old woman then walked my way.

She gave me a smile as she pushed her cart.
I knew right away that this was the start.
Let me push that for you.
And when we get to your car, I'll help you there, too.

We loaded the groceries into the back.
I subdued her with chloroform then drove to the shack.
When I dragged her inside she started to wake
And when she saw my claws she started to shake.

I'd never drawn them on anyone before.
With my hands ready to strike, I still wasn't sure.
Finish her off. Rip her heart from her chest.
Father stood in the door, then we'll clean up your mess.

I just couldn't do it; I sobbed and I cried.
But father made sure that the old woman died.
We ate her in silence, father didn't speak.
I knew what he was thinking; that I was too weak.

I contemplated from my bed, was I a beast or a mouse?
Then someone knocked at the door of the house.
It was a woman and a man; Amy and Tom.
She said she was looking for her missing mom.

Someone spotted her car not far from here.
You haven't seen her, have you, my dear?
After a moment, I shook my head "no".
I'm sorry, Amy and Tom, but you both have to go.

Father isn't awake, and he will get mad.
Everyone knows he's not really your dad.
Leave right now and never come back.
I wanted Amy hung up in the shack.

Her words had greatly wounded my pride.
My beast just couldn't let those words from her slide.
I plotted and planned; I wanted her heart.
Blood-soaked claws would tear her apart.

Up the stairs I sprinted to my father's bed,
Screaming out loud that I wanted her dead.

Father comforted me closely, who cares what they say?
For we are the beasts and they are the prey.

It was nice to once again hear father speak.
The silence had lasted for nearly a week.
As tears fell from my eyes, his hug helped me cope.
There in his words, he hadn't given up hope.

Amy and Tom hired a P.I.
It was as if they were begging to die.
Out by the trees, poking out of the ground,
He found the car then the cops came around.

They asked father questions and he answered them clear.
When they all left, he said, there's nothing to fear.
They don't have evidence or any proof.
But until this is over, we'll stay under our roof.

The police were gathering facts but they needed more.
They reviewed the footage they had from the store.
There on the cameras, in black and in white,
The old woman and me, there in plain sight.

They came with their sirens, their lights red and blue.
They came with their weapons; and their K-9s, too.
They scoured our property from the front to the back.
Amongst the trees, the police found the shack.

They found bones and blood and they found the chains.
They found what was left of our victims' remains.
They had all they needed to put us away.
They came to the house at the start of the day.

They surrounded the house when up came the sun.
My father and I had nowhere to run.
The windows; we made sure they were all blocked.
We barricaded the doors even though they were locked.

Father and I were upstairs in my room,
Both of us awaited our impending doom.
Father sat me down on my bed,
Very quietly he whispered, soon, I'll be dead.

I know I've been difficult, I know I've been stern.
But they were all lessons you needed to learn.
Everything that I gave you was all I could give.
Only one of us now is destined to live.

Jump from your window, and float on the breeze.
When you land on your feet, make a dash for the trees.
Without hesitation and without a sound,
I leapt from the window and landed on the ground.

Bullets rang out and from the roof spewed smoke.
From out the front door spilled the cops with a choke.
From the edge of the yard I watched the house burn.
For the next year, for revenge I would yearn.

As an adult I was homeless again.
I hadn't lived on the street since I was ten.
Late one night, when it was dark,
I met a young couple in a small park.

I had made a bench into a bed.
The poor young couple; they thought I was dead.
The pregnant woman asked, are you alright?
I replied, yes. You can't sleep here tonight.

Come to our home, there's plenty of space.
You can sleep in our nursery until you find your own place.
For that to happen, I'm going to need work.
We own a small shop, and you can be clerk.

Why would you help me? I'm no one to you.
That's where you're wrong. I was homeless once, too.

When we pulled up to their house, I felt intense.
It was a luxurious home behind a white picket fence.

Once inside, they gave me a tour.
It was a beautiful place with an addictive allure.
The nursery was a magical sight,
All the décor was especially bright.

It had pink painted walls, and a white carpet floor,
With painted hearts on the windows and door.
A smile crossed my face from ear to ear.
I think that you will be comfortable here.

For a little while I was very happy there.
I slept every night without any care.
The job was easy; there were many happy faces.
We went out to eat at the most expensive places.

None of the food was ever as sweet,
As the victims who screamed as I chewed on their meat.
The blood I consumed was replaced by the wine
That I drank from a glass, but often a stein.

Getting lost in the booze was the only way
I survived every night, or faced every day.
My father, whom I could never forget,
Dwelled on my mind with each ounce of regret.

No matter how much or times that I lied,
I knew I was the reason that my father died.
Because all of my happiness had slipped away,
I told the pregnant woman that I couldn't stay.

A disappointed frown covered her face.
Please reconsider leaving our place.
Take a day to decide. Maybe take two.
We will support whatever you do.

I told her I'd take one night or maybe take two,
Before I decided just what I would do.
Lying in bed, and still wide awake,
I contemplated whether leaving would be a mistake.

That's when I heard a very loud clang,
So I went to investigate what made that loud bang.
Tip-toeing to the basement I heard a low voice.
The words confirmed staying was a very bad choice.

She'll stay with us until we tear a baby from her womb.
And down here, in this basement, will be her dark tomb.
In the corner of the basement was a small cage.
When the man saw me, his eyes filled with rage.

With a quick strike, he grabbed my arm.
His words and his face; he meant to do harm.
As I attempted to fight the man's grip,
The woman just stared, and then I noticed it.

Looking at her belly, the bump it was gone.
This was their game and I was their pawn.
As he dragged me to the cage, it started to make sense.
My feelings of fear and dread were intense.

He slammed the door shut on my tiny cell.
I took a deep breath and released a loud yell.
No one can hear you." The woman said with a sinister smile.
You can keep screaming, but after a while…

You will provide me and my husband with what I cannot.
You'll produce me a baby or in that cage you will rot.
I admitted to myself that I didn't see this twist.
I may be a beast, but monsters exist.

Night after night and day after day,
It all played out the very same way.

They'd drugged all the food they gave me to eat,
Then the man would rape me, and then I'd get beat.

Night after night became week after week.
The woman and I would never speak.
I would only ever see the man,
But they didn't know I was forming a plan.

If I summoned the strength to release my beast,
The man and the woman would be my feast.
Father had told me that it was my heart;
The reason my beast never tore humans apart.

It was too soft and it was too kind.
That's how I'd gotten myself into this bind.
But what I'd gone through had changed something inside.
The beast wanted out and it didn't want to hide.

When the man came to the basement for his nightly attack,
Without any fighting I laid on my back.
It was unusual for me to be such a mute,
But it didn't seem to bother the disgusting brute.

Instead of the tears, in silence I thought,
About my father and the joy that he brought.
I thought about Amy and I thought about Tom.
I thought about their delicious and dead old mom.

I thought about the P.I., the cops, and the pain.
I thought about how much I wanted to eat the man's brain.
When through the basement window, I saw the moon,
Everything at once was finally in tune.

First it was my claws that I unsheathed.
Next I revealed my razor-sharp teeth.
The smell of his blood was very divine.
Every ounce in his body; it would be mine.

His neck was right there in front of my eyes.
I sunk my teeth in, to his surprise.
His blood sprayed my face but it was only a tease.
My claws stabbed his stomach and that made him freeze.

My beast shredded him easily and it was a thrill.
Tearing his head from his torso, I made my very first kill.
Creeping upstairs, down on all fours,
I crawled through hallways and peaked around doors.

Slithering through the house, moving like a snake,
I headed for the bedroom where the bitch I'd awake.
Mounting her in silence, I revealed my claws.
Sharpened fangs ready to taste her, but her eyes made me pause.

They begged me for mercy; I could see it on her face.
Where once there was her heart, my fist took its place.
A buffet of her across a blood-stained sheet.
The taste of the woman just couldn't be beat.

I ingested every organ, every muscle, and then,
With a full belly, I sauntered to the den.
After snatching car keys from the desk, and a wallet of cash,
Out the front door I made a quick dash.

I drove their car far and I drove their car fast.
The meal in my belly; well it wouldn't last.
Although I had eaten their flesh galore,
Before the sun rose, I would need more.

Starved and deprived to say the least,
I drove the car west and I drove the car east.
Needing to satisfy my appetite,
Hunting for food was such a delight.

I fed on an asshole who continued to yell,
At a girl who screamed: "Bitch! Go to Hell!"

I devoured a homeless man racked with despair.
He let me chew on him without any care.

They were both appetizers; morsels not men.
I needed a main course and to feed again.
There was a blonde woman who looked very sad.
The voice on her phone sounded very mad.

She was crying and upset; her tears would be seasoning.
She was uncontrollably frantic and beyond all reasoning.
A friend tried to comfort her and grabbed hold of her arm.
Come home with me before you do any harm.

The woman refused and jumped in her car.
All of it unfolded in front of a bar.
Both of us sped through the tense night,
Flooring it under every single red light.

She should have noticed me, at least you would think.
Perhaps she had a little too much to drink.
When she pulled into her driveway, I parked across the street.
Her home looked like it was innocent and sweet.

She stumbled to the front door with wobbling knees,
And angrily searched in her pockets for keys.
She was a mess and ugh, her poor heart.
There was no way I could rip her apart.

Or perhaps, she was depressed, and wished to be slain.
Either way, I could see all of her pain.
She opened the door and then headed inside.
In her backyard I found a dark place to hide.

Through a large window, I anticipated and stared.
When I saw the blonde woman, I was hardly prepared.
She wasn't upset, or crying at all.
She was happy, laughing, and smiling at a wall.

The wall was white, and void of décor.
Why was she smiling? I wasn't sure.
A table next to the blonde woman held a small tray,
Where paints of various colors there was an array.

Beside the paint palette was a large water bowl.
Closer to the window, I took a slow stroll.
I was mesmerized and curious; intrigued to say the least.
I needed answers before she met my beast.

When she got home, I thought she would faint.
Instead this blonde woman decided to paint.
And with her fingers?! I thought as she smeared
The paint on the wall as she laughed and she cheered.

The blonde woman painted with blue and with green.
She finger painted the most beautiful scene.
It was a grassy field with flowers and trees,
Whose limbs came to life with a light gentle breeze.

Swipes with white paint represented the air.
She painted the scene with the utmost of care.
It made me wish somehow, and some way,
That I was there with father on that hot sunny day.

I forced open the back door and it swung with a squeak.
I snuck inside the house for a much closer peak.
The painted wall was more beautiful than I could have dreamed.
My smile faded when the blonde woman screamed.

I'm not going to hurt you. You're not going to die.
I have several questions and I want to know why.
Why did you paint after leaving the bar?
You followed me home?! Yes, in my car.

You were upset and I watched you leave.
I had an argument with my ex-husband, Steve.

You were crying, and it seemed you were sad.
After painting the wall, you're not, and I'm glad.

Painting helps me when I'm feeling depressed.
When I'm painting this wall I'm no longer stressed.
That's when I told her about Amy and Tom.
That's when I told her about their dead mom.

I told her about father and I told her about the shack.
I told her about the pregnant woman and the man and the attack.
That I ate an asshole I saw on the street,
But on his bones was very little meat.

That I chewed on a homeless man full of despair.
He let me chew and that he didn't care.
I told her inside of me that there is a beast.
That it is starving and that it must feast.

But watching her paint was more satisfying,
Than watching my victims scream while they were dying.
Watching you paint, it was a rush.
I was surprised when you didn't use a brush.

Painting with fingers isn't as taxing.
Try it yourself and you'll find it's relaxing.
My favorite color is a shade of blue.
It's there on the palette in a beautiful hue.

With wet fingers I stroked the wall,
And made a new painting out of it all.
The grassy field was gone from my sight,
As I scribbled and scribbled to my heart's delight.

As I painted, I heard her phone ring.
She glanced at it quickly and didn't say a thing.
The look in her eyes was familiar to me.
The sadness and depression were easy to see.

She told me about Steve and how he abused her.
She wanted him nightly but he would refuse her.
The blonde woman discovered that Steve had been cheating.
How finding that out was very defeating.

Now Steve calls, he brags and he flaunts,
About his new girlfriend and continuously taunts.
For the blonde woman there was no reprieve.
She was constantly harassed by her ex-husband Steve.

Is Steve heavy or is Steve thin?
Steve has gained weight. And he has a double chin.
It sounds like Steve is more than a snack.
I'll eat him really quick, and then I'll come back.

No! she screamed, and then grabbed my arm.
I don't want you to do Steve any harm.
I'm going to eat Steve so the abuse will end.
I'm going to eat him because you're my friend.

Your focus is pointed in the wrong direction.
Amy and Tom should be your obsession.
I haven't forgotten about Amy and Tom.
I haven't forgotten about their dead mom.

I have something special for them in mind.
But it includes others that I cannot find.
The sheriff, two deputies and the P.I.
All together at once they all must die.

You broke into my house but now you're my guest.
I believe I can help you in your vicious quest.
In front of a computer, in her den,
I searched the web for the names of the men.

I had every name with the flick of my wrist.
Beside the computer, I made a short list:

Sherriff Peters, Deputy Wilson, and Deputy Bly.
Amy and Tom Andrews, and McNally, the P.I.

The Sheriff was the very first name.
After father died, he rose to fame.
He was promoted, transferred and left his wife.
Sheriff Peters had created a whole new life.

But no matter how far or long he could run,
He'd never escape the damage he'd done.
He gave the order and sent in his men.
After I ate him, he'd give no orders again.

Deputy Wilson's wife is pregnant with their third.
A happy family for him isn't deserved.
He's the one that shot father and for that he must pay.
I'd make sure Deputy Wilson didn't get away.

Deputy Wilson is invited over for dinner.
After which he'll be a lot thinner.
Nothing could be done about Deputy Bly,
The other deputy that I wanted to die.

He was Wilson's partner, confidant and friend.
Unfortunately for us both, Bly met his end.
His car ran a stop light and it hit another.
He died on the scene but not his brother.

His brother was ejected and bloodied his face.
His brother would have to take Bly's place.
McNally, John McNally, he was the P.I.
A slob of a man that was addicted to pie.

He ate and he ate until he couldn't any more.
He had grown so large he couldn't fit through a door.
Not that there's anything wrong with that,
He lived all alone, all except for his cat.

No more investigating, no more wrecked lives.
All alone with himself, his cat, and his pies.
Who could forget about Amy and Tom?
Or the sweet taste of their precious dead mom?

They had an apartment on the upper eastside.
It was easy to find just where they reside.
They're adult twins living together; but I didn't care.
I'd go to their place and hope they'd be there.

I want them to see me, I don't give a damn.
I want them to see me and know who I am.
With the information compiled, I spun around.
The blonde woman, however, could not be found.

She wasn't in the kitchen, in the bathroom or her bed.
She hid in the hallway closet crying instead.
That's where I found her, scared and alone.
She attempted to dial the police on her phone.

I tore it from her, and revealed my sharp claws.
I slashed her throat open without any pause.
After resting all day, I drove down the block.
Then stood at the sheriff's front door and gave it a knock.

When the door swung open, I was no longer there.
Neither was Sheriff Peters, to be honest and fair.
It was a teenage girl, and not the sheriff or wife.
There was more to Sheriff Peters and his new life.

Moving to the backyard, across freshly mowed grass,
I approached the patio door and tapped on the glass.
Into the shadows I disappeared,
When the face of the teenager again reappeared.

She opened the door with fear and with fright,
She screamed who's there into the night.

She held onto the door as I watched and I waited.
Then the sheriff appeared and he seemed agitated.

No one is outside! Now go back to bed!
You're getting all worked up with all of this dread!
Her fear made my tender face smile,
Something it hadn't done in a while.

The sheriff slammed the door and turned off the light.
I crept toward the house as they vanished from sight.
It was an overwhelming feeling,
When I entered their house, and crouched on the ceiling.

Very slowly I made my way down the hall,
As I tapped my fingers against the thin wall.
The sheriff stormed out of his room with a bat.
I didn't hear it before, but I did hear that!

He said to the teenager, who clung to his side.
There's somebody here and they're trying to hide!
When those words spilled from his mouth I knew it was time,
I jumped down in front of him and it was sublime.

I wanted to say who I was and to gloat,
Instead I grabbed them both by the throat.
Deputy Wilson took his dog out for a walk,
Down his dark road while on his phone he did talk.

With the conversation with his wife occupying his mind,
I followed him closely a few steps behind.
Deputy? I whispered and said with a grin,
Then knelt behind a bush as he turned with his chin.

He stopped in his tracks and looked all around,
But my innocent face just couldn't be found.
What's wrong? I heard say a voice on the phone.
Nothing, my dear. I'm on my way home.

He walked a little further and to his surprise,
I revealed myself and then we locked eyes.
That's such a nice dog, but he'd be happier with me.
I unclipped his leash and set the dog free.

I'm a lover of animals, but I really loved my dad.
Deputy Wilson, you know that you've been bad.
You're the little girl; the one from the fire!
To have you for dinner is what I desire.

I leapt at the deputy and jumped on his back.
The dog whimpered and whined as he watched the attack.
Deputy Bly's brother was the survivor.
Deputy Bly's brother was a paid driver.

I hailed him from the sidewalk and he gave me a ride.
It was quite comfortable when I hopped inside.
I could tell from his face that he had been crying.
He told me about the accident and his brother dying.

He said it was his fault because he'd been drinking.
He was drunk out of his mind and just wasn't thinking.
He called his brother because he needed a ride.
If he hadn't been drinking his brother wouldn't have died.

It's not your fault that your brother is dead.
If you had driven, it would have been you instead.
I'd rather it had been. I have no reason to live.
I gave everything to others that I had to give.

It's left me feeling lifeless, empty and alone.
I drive this car all night so I don't have to go home.
Inside my apartment, my thoughts dance in my mind.
When I'm at home, it's impossible to unwind.

But driving this car and meeting kind people like you,
Helps me feel happy and not to feel blue.

I just couldn't do it; his brother didn't have to die.
I'm glad it wasn't him and it was Deputy Bly.

It wasn't me that killed him, but dead is still dead.
My stop, my house, is just up ahead.
At the blonde woman's porch I waved the taxi goodbye.
I thought about what he told me, and on the porch I did cry.

I went to go see McNally, John McNally, the P.I.
I knocked on his door while holding a pie.
When he didn't answer, well I knocked again.
After three or four knocks I heard movement within.

He answered the door and his eyes saw the pie.
With a fake smile I told him my lie.
This fresh dessert was baked just for you.
Somebody ordered it. Don't ask me who.

What flavor is it? Does it have whipped cream?
It's a strawberry pie, and it tastes like a dream.
He tore the pie from my hands and then slammed the door.
If you enjoy that pie, I'll bring you some more!

I wanted him to enjoy it and taste every bit.
Under layers of berries there's a layer of shit.
Mixed into the pie was a very strong drug.
It left him unconscious; passed out on a rug.

He was drooling and pie was all over his face.
I'd never get him to the blonde woman's place.
All I could do is watch him and stare.
So I sank my teeth in and ate him right there.

It was finally time to visit Amy and Tom,
And remind them who killed their poor dead mom.
Following them from their place on the upper eastside,
It was a short, and sweet, and joyful ride;

We traveled to the grocery store where I met their mom.
In the same parking lot, I saw Amy and Tom.
After grabbing a cart, and heading into the store,
We walked past each other while in aisle four.

Both of their faces had a blank stare,
They didn't know who I was, or they didn't care.
When we all stood together in the checkout line,
Their cart full of groceries was right in front of mine.

Had I grown so much that I didn't look the same?
Did they remember the house, my father, my name?
Beside their car I asked, do you know who I am?
I'm sorry, we're busy, and we don't give a damn.

Let me help you remember. Then I showed them my claws.
I drove them into Tom's shoulder and that made Amy pause.
Now you remember that sweet little child?
Once I was young, so meek and so mild.

That child is gone and now I am the beast.
Both of you are invited to my special feast.
With Tom's blood spilled all over her blouse,
I forced Amy to drive to the blonde woman's house.

As we sat in the driveway with Tom in the back,
I gave Amy chloroform and she faded to black.
There was a very large table in a brightly lit room,
Where each of my victims awaited their doom.

Sheriff Peters, Deputy Wilson, Amy and Tom; all in chains.
On a plate, on the table, sat the P.I.'s brains.
As you look around at each other's face,
You all know why you're here in this place.

My father, you killed. My house, you burned.
All of you taught me a lesson I've learned.

Never again will I be friendly, soft or kind.
My eyes are now open when once they were blind.

Now here we are at this very late hour.
All of your hearts I'll soon devour.
McNally, John McNally, has already died.
Those are his brains there by your side.

You may not have known, but he was addicted to pie.
I'm addicted to killing, and now you must die.
I ripped the sheriff's throat out in a blink,
And then had a cup of his warm blood to drink.

All of the others began to scream,
As I licked his guts from my fingers like cream.
I laughed as I punched Deputy Wilson through the heart.
Then jumped on the table after I tore him apart.

I was drenched in blood from my toes to my head.
He shot my father so I'm glad that he's dead!
I squatted on the table in front of Amy and Tom.
It was me; I kidnapped your poor, sweet mom!

I threw her into the car with the groceries in the back.
While she was unconscious, I drove to the shack.
That's when we ate her and she tasted so sweet.
The flesh of your mother was quite a treat.

I kicked Amy and Tom over and they crashed to the floor.
I want to eat you two, and I want to eat you more;
More than the sheriff, the deputy or the P.I.
I want to eat you two and then watch you die!

I'm going to eat you slowly, no matter the taste.
I won't let any piece of you go to waste.
Down on my knees I peeled the skin from Tom's chest.
I carved him wide open, and then took a short rest.

I dug at him slowly, like a hole in the sand.
Tom was in pieces with the wave of my hand.
Holding a chunk of his flavorful meat,
I sunk my teeth in and his eyes watched me eat.

I chewed and I chewed until I couldn't no more,
Then spit his bits out all over the floor.
I sat on Amy's chest as I saved her for last.
I'll never forget what she said in the past.

Not my real father? You were so very wrong.
Just like my father, I am now strong.
I'll do as he did and I'll feast and I'll feast.
No one in this world is safe from my beast!

I sliced and I diced, and slowly cut her up like a ham.
Now you'll never forget who I am!
I ate a piece of her arm, her stomach and her leg.
If you want me to stop eating, I want you to beg!

Please! I'm sorry! Just let me die!
I ate another piece and then I told her, goodbye!
I slashed her throat open and the blood flowed like wine.
Though she was dead I continued to dine.

When I was full, I staggered down the hall,
And into the room where I had painted the wall.
Though I was dizzy, and thought I might faint,
I dipped my bloody fingers into some paint.

Write a Sad Poem:

Write a Happy Poem:

Write a Love Poem:

Write an Inspirational Poem:

OUT OF THE DARKNESS

A Book Of Poetry

By

Brian M. King

115